METHUEN PLAYSCRIPTS

The Methuen Playscripts series exists
to publish scripts of plays which have
not yet become widely known but which
have already earned themselves a place
in the acting repertoire of the modern
theatre.

TRANSCENDING and THE DANCERS

These two one-act plays were written
as a double bill but their subjects are
quite independent. They are the work
of one of the most promising of the new
British playwrights.

TRANSCENDING is a fast-moving and
farcical psychological drama in mini-
ature about a girl who fails her A levels.
The problem of her future is viewed
with varying degrees of calm and
hysteria by her mother and father and
two neighbours: her own solution is
logical if unexpected.

"Mr Cregan is a born theatrical
entertainer..."
John Russell Taylor in
Plays & Players

The point of departure for THE
DANCERS is a celebration party.
"Archetypal absurdities of human
nature are produced in abandon, rather
like a cascade of glistening soap bubbles,
to be punctured with infinite precision
by needles of wit .... (Mr Cregan)
has added the original adjunct of com-
plementary mood music, ranging from
Wagner for instant tension to Palm
Court for soothing the savage breast
and Strauss for making whoopee in the
Vienna Woods."
Glasgow Herald

OTHER METHUEN PLAYSCRIPTS

Paul Ableman	TESTS
Barry Bermange	NATHAN AND TABILETH and OLDENBERG
Edward Bond	SAVED
Kenneth H. Brown	THE BRIG
David Campton	LITTLE BROTHER : LITTLE SISTE and OUT OF THE FLYING PAN
Henry Chapman	YOU WON'T ALWAYS BE ON TOP
David Cregan	THREE MEN FOR COLVERTON
John McGrath	EVENTS WHILE GUARDING THE BOFORS GUN

A METHUEN PLAYSCRIPT

Transcending

The Dancers

DAVID CREGAN

First published in Great Britain 1967
by Methuen & Co Ltd
11 New Fetter Lane, London, E.C.4

Printed in Great Britain by
Lowe & Brydone (Printers) Ltd
London

AUTHOR'S NOTE

I wrote Transcending as a curtain raiser to The Dancers, intending both plays to have the same cast, which I think is possible. Experience indicates that, if the plays are done as a double bill, The Dancers should actually be played first. Both plays should be done clearly and simply.

Transcending depends on speed. At the Royal Court the actors ran to their places between scenes like automata, to the rhythm of a delightful piece of music by Robert Long. The use of blackouts at these points is likely to slow the pace very badly, and any pause detracts from the feeling of slight hysteria the play generates. Please note that the transposition of speeches towards the end of Scene Two is intentional.

The Dancers has no set. I believe it should be performed on a white floor, with the changing light as a pervasive background, like a cocoon. The light changes are important, and will be seen in performance as a choric comment, sometimes at odds with the action, sometimes in sympathy with some or all of the characters. The music, on the other hand, produces instant atmosphere. Brimley should dress in cheap smart clothes; Martin should dress in a sports jacket (in Edinburgh he was effectively given the button-down B.B.C. look); Mr Bowhorn (bow as in tie) suggests a summer jacket; Miss Partlip suggests a hat and a white or flowery dress; Mrs Faraclough always seemed to me to wear long clothes, like an Edwardian madam, though a black 'twenties' cocktail dress was extremely effective at The Court. Martin's fancy dress must be huge, perhaps like a great sunflower painted by a child. Buskins would help it.

'Meanings' have been sought in these plays. Works of art, it sometimes seems, are codes to be cracked, or sugared sermons to be laid bare, which is a sterile thought. Transcending strikes me as an obvious joke, and The Dancers as an obvious struggle. At its simplest, this struggle can be said to twitch and snarl among The Certain, The Uncertain and The Effete. However, a director, and his audience, should concentrate on the people and the pace rather than the abstractions. Only Brimley, after all, is really aware of what he is doing.

Although I am indebted to Gordon McDougall of The Traverse Theatre, Edinburgh, for a delightful and heartening production of The Dancers in November 1966, which allowed me to cut the play considerably, I am especially indebted to the original casts at The Royal Court whose generosity gave these plays their first life. Most of all I am grateful to Jane Howell, to whom these published versions are dedicated.

TRANSCENDING and THE DANCERS were first performed
by the English Stage Company as a Production Without Decor
at the Royal Court Theatre on Sunday, January 23rd, 1966,
with the following cast:

TRANSCENDING

GIRL	Barbara Ferris
FATHER	Bernard Gallagher
MOTHER	Jean Boht
SIMON	Ronald Pickup
MR LEMSTER	Roger Booth

THE DANCERS

MR BOWHORN	Peter Wyatt
MARTIN	Davyd Harries
MISS PARTLIP	Gillian Martell
MRS FARACLOUGH	Frances Cuka
BRIMLEY	Joseph Greig

Directed by Jane Howell
Designed by Charles Knode
Music for TRANSCENDING by Robert Long

TRANSCENDING went into the repertoire at the Royal Court
with Keith Johnstone's THE PERFORMING GIANT on
Thursday, March 3rd, Roddy Maude-Roxby playing the part
of Simon.

TRANSCENDING

The scene is a single room with a door at the back and a door stage left going outside. The room contains a table, two chairs, and a divan bed. The bed should be easily covered or hidden.

The room area and the area outside the door can be lit separately. Some scenes take place in the dark.

SCENE ONE

FATHER reading a paper at the table. The GIRL enters the outside area and addresses the audience. Until the end of the play she wears a raincoat.

GIRL: That door is the door to our house. I've been out late because I didn't want to tell my father I've failed A levels again. It's the third time. I've been out since early morning, but there isn't much hope that he'll think I've been in bed all day with a cold, so I'm going to have to face him. There's bound to be a row.

(She goes into the room.)

Hullo, Dad.

FATHER: Failed again, have you?

GIRL: That's right.

FATHER: Never mind.

GIRL: Now don't get excited, Dad. It's only an exam.

FATHER: Yes.

GIRL: The job I get they'll be glad I failed.

FATHER: What job's that?

GIRL: Now don't worry, Dad. I'll get on.

FATHER: Ought I to worry?

GIRL: No. And don't bring up Mr Lemster.

FATHER: He said you were going to fail.

GIRL (to the audience): This probably means a fight. Mr Lemster's a medium, a good one.

(To FATHER): You're angry, aren't you?

FATHER (surprised): No.

GIRL: You are!

A*

FATHER: I'm not!

GIRL: Don't shout, Dad, please. You're just upset, that's all.

FATHER: Upset?

GIRL: I tried for that exam, I really tried. I did just what the teachers told me to.

FATHER: They told you wrong, then.

GIRL: You might have sent me to a school you respected.

FATHER: Mr Lemster said you'd fail, and you believed him. That's all.

(MOTHER calls from off stage, back.)

MOTHER: Is she back?

GIRL (to the audience): My mother.

MOTHER: Is she?

GIRL: Yes, Mum.

(MOTHER enters.)

MOTHER: Darling!

(She clasps her daughter.)

Oh my darling, I'm so sorry!

GIRL: It's all right, Mum.

MOTHER: You're not to worry yourself about it all, or you'll make yourself ill and have a break down.

GIRL (to the audience): I'll have to cheer my mother up now. She's set her heart on a degree.

MOTHER: Exams, after all, what are exams? People fail them all the while and the world still goes round.

GIRL: I can't go to the university.

MOTHER: That's a relief, darling. That's how you ought to look on that piece of news. You can get straight on with some work. Oh darling, you mustn't be disappointed.

GIRL: Now, Mum, you mustn't worry about it. I'll get a job.

MOTHER: Of course you will, poor thing.

FATHER: I'm going to bed.

(FATHER goes off at the back.)

MOTHER: Let's have a heart to heart and get it straight.

GIRL: All right.

MOTHER: You can cry if you want to.

GIRL: I'll try.

MOTHER: Now tell me everything and I'll just sit and understand.

GIRL (to the audience): This always happens.

SCENE TWO

The GIRL is standing in the outside area.

GIRL (to the audience): This is Simon's place. Next door. Simon's quite remote from me, and I couldn't bear him to be any other way. I think he's thirty-one. The attraction of an older man is that of the ultimate risk. Anything could happen. So far, Simon hasn't touched me.

(She knocks.)

Hullo.

(Silence.)

(To the audience): He likes to keep me in suspense. Hullo!

SIMON (from the divan bed): Who is it?

GIRL: Me.

SIMON: Go away.

GIRL: I want to talk to you.

SIMON: At this hour?

GIRL: Yes.

SIMON (getting up in pyjamas): You know what I'm going to say.

GIRL (to the audience): He's so strong. I take all my troubles to him and he never weakens.

SIMON (putting on the light): I'm going to tell you to face the facts. You never like that, do you?

GIRL: It gives me a frisson.

(SIMON opens the door. The GIRL walks into the room. SIMON closes the door.)

SIMON: You've failed your A levels again.

GIRL: I love the way you crush me, Simon. Right out you crush me so there's no hope for me at all.

SIMON: That's that done, then. Goodnight.

(He switches off the light and goes to bed. Stage in darkness.)

GIRL: Simon.

SIMON: No, I know it doesn't matter that you've failed A levels again. But what about a job? Oh, you're going to get a job, and not just any job but a special job, a personality job, like a receptionist or a private secretary, or an assistant to a research scientist. Good. Do you think you can get that kind of job? Yes. And you can get one tomorrow if you want. Good. Very good. Good night.

(The GIRL switches on the light.)

GIRL (to the audience): You see? With an older man there are no punches pulled. When he hurts you, he hurts you very badly indeed. We're lucky in our neighbour.

(She switches light out. Stage in darkness.)

SIMON: You meant to fail those A levels.

GIRL: Simon.

SIMON: I've known it all along.

GIRL: You read my mind like a book.

SIMON: You're just predictable, that's all.

(Silence.)

Well? What've you got to say to that?

(Silence.)

I said what've you got to say to that?

(Silence.)

Oh Lord.

(He gets up and switches on the light. The room is empty. The GIRL is standing outside the door.)

Now for the mother.

(He goes out at the back.)

GIRL (to the audience): I can't face the truth. It's been my trouble for years, of course, and it's affected my intellect. It's affected everything, actually, as you can see. Of course, I know I can't face the truth, but it doesn't make any difference. I enjoy it really, like when Simon crushes me. But even he goes too far in the end and I have to leave. That's nice for my mother, though, because she can always judge when I've left and then dash round for a scene with him. We all like to help one another. She loves drama, my mother.

(She moves back to be out of sight of her mother. MOTHER rushes on in an outdoor coat.)

MOTHER (battering on the door): Simon! Simon! For God's sake let me in, Simon!

(Enter SIMON with two cups without saucers.)

SIMON: All right, all right, all right.

MOTHER: Is that you, Simon?

SIMON: Of course.

MOTHER: Thank God.

(SIMON opens the door.)

SIMON: What is it?

MOTHER: Is she here?

SIMON: No.

MOTHER: She must be!

SIMON: Why?

MOTHER: Two cups.

SIMON: Me and you.

MOTHER: For God's sake, Simon, has she been?

SIMON: Yes.

MOTHER: Thank God.

(She collapses in a chair.)

SIMON: Why?

MOTHER: She's still alive.

SIMON: She might not be by now.

MOTHER: Oh yes, she is.

GIRL (to the audience): If she thought I'd kill myself she'd have to go away and look for me, and that would spoil it for her.

MOTHER: She's so lucky you're a neighbour Simon. You always give her that confidence her father doesn't seem able to generate.

SIMON (quite straightforwardly): I give her the security of knowing someone cares for her, someone - it may seem a funny thing to say - loves her. No Simon, don't deny it, you love her somehow, in a funny kind of way, and, I don't know, but as I watch you struggling with yourself, I see you, too, a lonely boy at bottom, and in my woman's heart I know that deep down you need her as much as she needs you.

MOTHER: I don't need any one.

SIMON: Oh yes you do. We all need someone, Simon, for nobody's an island and sufficient unto himself.

MOTHER: You stupid old woman. You don't know what you're saying, do you. It's just an excuse for histrionics to you.

SIMON: Don't scorn a woman's instinct, Simon. We know. And Simon, I'm artistic and have that special knowledge. It's not a virtue, Simon, it's a gift. The way I'm made.

GIRL (to the audience): She can't help exploiting a situation. Simon doesn't go for situations. They ruin communication. Communication is Simon's big thing. You'd wonder how I failed A levels, wouldn't you, being so bright.

MOTHER: But Simon, she communicates to me. As I tell her all the time, I'm on her wavelength.

SIMON: Her situation is one which family units typically produce-

(MOTHER and SIMON speak together against each other.)

in which communication is impossible because of the intolerable strain of knowing the emotional pressures that lie behind each remark. She can't communicate directly, none of us can. That's the whole tragedy of the human race, that we can't say what's inside us because we don't know how, and because others won't listen, and because to communicate we have to break taboos.

MOTHER (speaking at the same time as the previous speech)

Oh Simon, you silly boy, what do you know about the ties and loves a mother and her daughter have between them? You can't imagine that the placental bond is severed just like that, or that we haven't got an instinct, just as you men have, to recognise things in each other that the opposite sex knows nothing whatever about. And artistic temperaments lead one to see so much.

(The GIRL walks away as they talk.)

SCENE THREE

The GIRL is standing in the outside area.

GIRL (to the audience): This door is where Mr Lemster lives.

(Calls): Mr Lemster!

(To audience): He'll only tell me that 2 a.m. is ridiculously late and that he doesn't want to see me. Then he'll find me rather too attractive to keep out, since he's a widower, and misses making love, and also has no children. There'll be a fight between his instincts on the one hand and his bachelor habits on the other, and eventually he'll let me in. Now I've told you that, there's not much point in your seeing it.

SCENE FOUR

FATHER seated in pyjamas by the table. MOTHER is taking off her outdoor coat. She continues to undress.

MOTHER: That boy Simon worries me. He's no ideals, no subtlety. Subtlety is everything to the artist. Where would Michelangelo have been without subtlety? It's the little touches, you know. A little touch of someone in the night.

FATHER: Harry.

MOTHER: And when I think of that poor girl roaming the streets, her future shattered, her personality seared by failing A levels, my heart bleeds. As if a person's soul could be reached by an exam.

FATHER: It wasn't her soul, they wanted, it was facts.

MOTHER: What are facts?

FATHER: It's half past two.

MOTHER: She'll be with Mr Lemster now.

FATHER: Is that all right?

MOTHER: She must learn to decide things for herself.

FATHER: But does she know the facts of life?

MOTHER: Facts! It's always facts, isn't it. Where's your imagination, your ideals, your subtlety?

FATHER: I think I'm worried. If she's upset, and gone to Mr Lemster, she ought to know the facts of life. And if she's not upset, she ought to know the facts of life anyway. And why's she gone to Mr Lemster? She's always gone to Mr Lemster. I'll tell you this. I'm going to see my daughter knows the facts of life!

SCENE FIVE

The GIRL is sitting on LEMSTER's knee by the table, listening to the telephone. LEMSTER is in pyjamas and dressing gown.

GIRL (into the phone): I did biology, you know, Dad, and just because I didn't pass it doesn't mean I didn't understand. Except one thing. How do you enjoy it? Well, people don't, do they. Psychology's all about people not enjoying it. Well, thanks for ringing, anyway. What? Oh he's... making some tea.

(She puts down the receiver.)

(To the audience):

That's the first time I've ever really heard him worried. I don't know that I can face it now it's happened.

LEMSTER: Have your exams upset him?

GIRL: Yes.

LEMSTER: I said you'd fail. It's hateful to see into the future and know the worst.

GIRL: He says you made me fail.

LEMSTER: I hope he's right, otherwise my future as a medium doesn't look too good.

GIRL (not moving): Well, I must go.

LEMSTER: You won't stay for tea?

GIRL: It won't stop at that, will it, and I won't do what you want.

LEMSTER: And yet you're fond of me.

GIRL: You're fond of me as well.

LEMSTER: I suppose I'm much too old.

GIRL: I like things as they are.

LEMSTER: Last night... Oh well, you won't be interested.

GIRL: A call came from the beyond about me. It came, funnily enough, about this time. What did it say?

LEMSTER: It said a secretarial college in the Cromwell Road is waiting for you.

GIRL: I'll see what happens.

(She gets off his knee.)

Goodnight.

(The GIRL goes out through the door, turns to the audience.)

It's really all too much, knowing the truth and knowing you can't face it. He's never been in touch with the Beyond in his life. The whole thing's absolutely phoney.

(She begins to cry.)

SCENE SIX

LEMSTER in his dressing gown still. FATHER in his overcoat, hat, and pyjama trousers. They are standing still, throwing things at each other - cups, saucers and plates. They stop.

LEMSTER: You've broken up my home.

FATHER: Only your china.

LEMSTER: You've broken up my china.

FATHER: Only some of it.

LEMSTER: You're a visionary, aren't you, trying to see into the heart of things.

FATHER (sits): I'd like to know one thing only, and it's not a mysterious thing. Why is life difficult? There's no reason I know of why life should be difficult but everybody I've ever heard of has found it so. Of course, the difficulties are relative. I'm not Prince Hamlet, for example.

LEMSTER: Quite.

FATHER: But despite a lifetime trying to find life easy, and I've made a very great effort as anyone will tell you, I've always ended up in difficulties.

LEMSTER: It's a question of words.

FATHER: Sometimes.

LEMSTER: And emotions.

FATHER: Sometimes.

LEMSTER: And intellect.

FATHER: Sometimes.

(Pause.)

Now why did you say I'd broken up your home when all you meant was I'd broken some of your china?

LEMSTER: Many reasons. First of all, I thought you wanted me to say it, because you'd come round here with that intention. You'd got up at 3 a.m., and come round here with the intention of breaking up my home.

FATHER: Why did I do that?

LEMSTER: Because of the influence I was having on your daughter.

FATHER: Let's examine that influence. Aspects. One, Supernatural. Two, Paternal. Three, Sexual.

LEMSTER: Let's examine the causes behind the sexual aspect. One, My Solitude. Two, Her Youth. Three, My Virility.

FATHER: We could tear away at it for hours. Let's get on with my motive.

LEMSTER: Broadly speaking you were impelled by envy, fear, and distrust of my influence, whatever it is, over your daughter, and came here to put an end to it. How better than by destroying my home?

FATHER: So I broke some of your china.

LEMSTER: Yes.

FATHER: And you wanted me to believe that in that puny action I was fulfilling my burning desire?

LEMSTER: Yes.

FATHER: Why?

LEMSTER: To please you.

FATHER: Why?

LEMSTER: To make you friendly towards me.

FATHER: To my mind, that's a very unsatisfactory reason for saying "You've broken up my home". Tell me another.

LEMSTER: I thought if I said "You've broken up my home" it would please your wife.

FATHER: Now that's interesting. It was partly at my wife's insistence that I came here.

LEMSTER: It always seemed a possibility.

FATHER: And in a way I was behaving like my wife in throwing the china.

LEMSTER: And I reacted to your wife in you by saying "You're breaking up my home".

FATHER: You see? Human motives are very obscure.

LEMSTER: Let's leave it at that.

FATHER: No. Many reasons you said, and we've only had two. We must have them all or they'll form an abcess of misunderstanding in my life.

LEMSTER: What d'you mean by life?

FATHER: Do I mean the passage of seconds during which I am conscious, or unconscious, or both, or do I mean the activities I have so far undertaken, or the whole sum of activities I will have undertaken by the time I die, or my evaluation of these activities? Or do I mean the force that keeps me alive, or the passage of time generally, including the passage of time that relates to me and my circle of friends, and their activities? Or do I mean my responses to external causes? Life has passed me by. You've saved my life.

LEMSTER: Life itself.

FATHER: That's life.

LEMSTER: Life is not a bowl of cherries.

FATHER: That's the only really confident definition there is. I'm trying to see myself vis-à-vis you.

LEMSTER: Well, shall I tell you what I want from your daughter?

FATHER: Let's try it.

LEMSTER: I would like first to have her as my mistress, second to have her as my daughter, and third to have her as a business partner to make me a successful medium.

FATHER: In that order?

LEMSTER: Take my advice and stick to that order and you'll find you make some progress.

SCENE SEVEN

SIMON in bed speaking into the telephone.

SIMON: It's 4 a.m.

No, people don't think more clearly at 4 a.m. It's a fallacy put out by those who find the daylight unromantic.

Salvation means subscribing to a moral doctrine opposed to the physical pleasures.

The soul doesn't exist as a separate entity at all. It's just an excuse for salvation.

Well, if you don't believe me...

Well, if you knew what I'd say...

Where are you?

I should try Westminster Abbey, then, if you want your prayers to stand a decent chance.

I'm not being flippant. I just believe in starting at the top.

You get down on your knees and say whatever you want to say. If I were you, I'd start with very simple sentences, because usually you say too much and muddle everyone.

Even Him.

Well, if He knows what's in your heart already, He's solved the problem of communication for you, hasn't He?

Yes, in the broadest sense of the word I'm a materialist. You've always known I'm a materialist.

I don't know if the Abbey's closed. I imagine it is. We all have to sleep sometime.

No, but His clergy do.

Well, kneel down on the floor of the telephone box then. Hullo.

Hullo.

Put the receiver back before you do it.

I say.

Hullo.

Hullo.

SCENE EIGHT

MOTHER, dressed in ordinary clothes, is putting breakfast on the table. FATHER marches in buttoning up his jacket, having obviously just got dressed.

FATHER (as he enters): The dirty old man wants my daughter to sleep with him.

MOTHER: No!

FATHER: Why not?

MOTHER (horrified): Why not?

FATHER: He's got good taste. You want to sleep with my daughter? Certainly. Fifty pounds.

MOTHER (horrified): What?

FATHER: A hundred pounds.

MOTHER: How dare you!

FATHER: Money doesn't enter into it, Mr Lemster. You

should respect the finer feelings of sex and take it for free.

MOTHER: He shouldn't take it at all!

FATHER: Ah! Caught you in an attitude! Now stick to it and we might get somewhere. Where's breakfast?

SCENE NINE

MR LEMSTER and SIMON both in outdoor coats, hats, and every appearance of daytime clothes, stand outside the door.

SIMON: No.

LEMSTER: Yes.

SIMON: No.

LEMSTER: Yes.

SIMON: No.

LEMSTER: Yes.

SIMON: No.

(Pause.)

LEMSTER: Politicians spend their lives avoiding this. It's confrontation.

SIMON: I don't want her to think my bed's a bed of lust.

LEMSTER: It's not the bed so much as the person in it.

SIMON: Not altogether. If she sleeps with you in my bed, she'll expect to sleep in it with me. It's a natural association, and I don't want it.

LEMSTER: But if you spend tonight in my bed, by association you'll want to go to bed with her terrifically.

SIMON: But if she's gone to bed with you she probably won't want to go to bed with me.

LEMSTER: But once I've been to bed in your bed, I mightn't want to go to bed with her at all.

SIMON: If she's in it already the urge might overcome the association.

LEMSTER: It would be an interesting experiment in suggestibility.

SIMON: It would.

LEMSTER: Shall we try?

SIMON: All right.

SCENE TEN

MOTHER and FATHER having breakfast. Lights on in the room.

FATHER (waving his fork at an imaginary LEMSTER): And if you feel paternal towards her, how d'you think I feel? Jealous is how I feel. Outraged because you want to deflower her, and jealous because you want to be her father. My God, you swine! You're tearing our family apart!

MOTHER (gesticulating as well): And you're a fraud as well.

FATHER (as above): A fraud who wants to fool the public at the expense of our daughter. Good God, I'll tell you this! I've never felt so much excitement in my life as I feel now! I've got you, and tonight I'm going to make it very clear you can't just mess around like this and get away with it.

MOTHER: Tonight we'll trap you in the act of lust, you filthy beast!

(She looks heavenward.)

Oh keep her safe from harm!

SCENE ELEVEN

Breakfast has gone. FATHER and MOTHER are exactly as they were.

FATHER: Thank goodness it's night. I thought the time would never pass.

MOTHER: Are you still angry?

FATHER: Yes.

(To the audience): I'm tired actually. We all are because

none of us slept at all last night.

(To MOTHER): I'll kill that Lemster, Mother!

MOTHER: Now be reasonable, darling.

FATHER: Reasonable!

(He laughs hollowly. To the audience): It's hard keeping everything in order. So long as my wife stays inflexible, I'll manage.

MOTHER: You mustn't do anything you'll regret, and remember, human life is sacred.

FATHER (slightly taken aback): You're not weakening?

MOTHER: I don't want blood on my husband's hands. I love him too much for that.

FATHER (to the audience): I can feel my energy going. The excitement's had its edge taken off.

(To MOTHER): Your daughter is in the hands of a filthy old seducer.

MOTHER: We must be tolerant.

FATHER: Tolerant?

MOTHER: Kind hearts are more than coronets, and simple faith than Norman blood.

FATHER: I've not worked hard all day to keep my energy and anger going full tilt to hear you saying that! I'm off to kill him! Now!

MOTHER (screams.)

FATHER (to the audience): That's it!

(He puts on his overcoat in great fury.)

MOTHER (to the audience): I've never seen him act like this before. It's an opportunity I could very well turn to my advantage.

(To FATHER): You're mad!

FATHER: Yes.

MOTHER: Remember your wife and children! Remember your loving friends! Remember.....

(FATHER goes outside, slamming the door.)

FATHER (to the audience): Done it. Now then, here goes.

(He goes off.)

SCENE TWELVE

MOTHER in her coat batters on the door from the outside.

MOTHER: Simon! Simon!

(To the audience): I've prepared the ground for ages and at last the climax has come. Many of us are born Cleopatras, you know, but society frustrates us. It's all the artistic temperament, really.

(She batters on the door.)

Simon! Simon!

(Sobs): You've got to let me in, Simon! Oh God, Simon! Simon, let me in!

(She batters and stops.)

LEMSTER (sitting up in the divan bed in his pyjamas and speaking to the audience): Now here's a curious thing. Is the young man carrying on with the mother?

MOTHER (batters): Simon!

LEMSTER: Suppose the daughter comes and finds me with her? One has to reckon up the profit and loss.

MOTHER (batters): Simon!

LEMSTER: When she was young, no-one took care of the younger generation like they do now, so she's getting pretty raddled.

MOTHER (batters): Simon!

LEMSTER: On the other hand, experience has advantages over youth.

(He gets up and goes towards the door.)

MOTHER: Simon!

LEMSTER: And a bird in the hand is worth two in the bush.

MOTHER: Murder! There's going to be a murder!

LEMSTER (opening the door and switching on the light in the room): Who of?

MOTHER: Oh!

LEMSTER: You're surprised?

MOTHER: Yes.

(To the audience): Well, what can I do? I'm all ready to

A**

go, after all.

(To LEMSTER): Surprised, and yet delighted.

(She embraces him and switches out the light as she does so. Stage in darkness.)

LEMSTER (pause): Well, who'd've thought it.

(MOTHER switches the light on.)

MOTHER (to the audience from his arms): It's rather Roman, isn't it, he being about to die.

(She switches the light out. The stage is in darkness. Silence. There is a knock on the door. Silence. There is a knock on the door again. Silence.)

GIRL (in the dark): Oh well, Simon, if that's how you feel I'm going to Mr Lemster.

(LEMSTER switches the light on. The GIRL has gone from outside the door.)

LEMSTER (pulling on his overcoat): I've got to go.

MOTHER: Why?

LEMSTER: I've got to be there to welcome her.

MOTHER: You mean I'm not the chicken you thought I was.

LEMSTER: I...

MOTHER: Oh no! My husband's right, I see that.

LEMSTER: What?

MOTHER: I hope he kills you as he said he would.

LEMSTER: Ah!

MOTHER: I begged him not to, but the impulse was upon him.

LEMSTER: Really?

MOTHER: Yes.

LEMSTER: Well, he has progressed. In that case...

(He moves with MOTHER towards the bed.)

SCENE THIRTEEN

FATHER in the area outside knocks on the door. He is in his overcoat and hat.

FATHER: Right, open up, you dirty dog. I'm after you.

SIMON (sitting up in divan bed, to the audience): How very peculiar.

FATHER: Come on. Let me in.

SIMON: What for?

FATHER (to the audience): Hullo. Orgies.

(To SIMON): I'm sending for the police, so you'd better hurry up.

SIMON (getting up, to the audience): Communication, you see. It's gone wrong again, and innocent people suffer as a result.

(He puts his dressing gown on over his pyjamas.)

FATHER: How many people have you got in there, Lemster?

(SIMON opens the door and switches on the light.)

Oh!

SIMON: Now what's the trick?

FATHER (entering): There isn't one. Where's Lemster?

(He is peering.)

SIMON: At my place.

FATHER: He wants to be my daughter's lover and I'm going to kill him.

SIMON: Why?

FATHER: Don't confuse things, Simon. I'm going to kill him and let's leave it there.

(The GIRL comes to door. She knocks. Silence. The GIRL knocks.)

FATHER (whispering): Who is it?

SIMON (whispering): It could be him.

FATHER (whispering): It could be her.

GIRL (calling): Mr Lemster.

FATHER (triumphant): Caught in the act.

SIMON: Who?

FATHER: No-one, I suppose. Hell's bells. I'd better go to your place.

(FATHER opens the door and strides off past the GIRL. SIMON goes to the door and looks at the GIRL.)

SIMON: Hullo.

(Silence.)

Would you like a cup of tea?

(The GIRL walks in and sits down.)

(To the audience): Association is an interesting phenomenon by which an idea is conveyed not by logic, but by, in fact, association. The idea that Lemster had in this bed has suddenly been conveyed to me in very startling terms.

(To the GIRL as he goes to the rear): I'll just put the kettle on.

(To the audience): Then we'll see if we can't come to some arrangement.

SCENE FOURTEEN

FATHER stands outside the door.

FATHER: This is Simon's place, only at the moment, apparently, Lemster's here. He'll tell me what a fool I am to have left Simon and my daughter alone together. He's probably right. That boy's sharp enough for anything.

SCENE FIFTEEN

FATHER stands outside the door.

FATHER: This is Lemster's place. Simon's never been interested in the girl before, so why should he be now? She's probably left him.

SCENE SIXTEEN

FATHER stands outside the door.

FATHER: This is Simon's place.

(He knocks.)

LEMSTER (from the divan bed where he is with MOTHER): Who is it?

FATHER: Me.

LEMSTER: Your daughter's looking for you. She's gone away.

(Pause.)

FATHER (to the audience): I must keep going somehow.

(He walks off. LEMSTER gets out of bed. He puts on the light. He begins putting on his overcoat over his pyjamas.)

MOTHER (in her petticoat on the bed): Put out the light and then put out the light. Our sins must be shrouded in the dark.

LEMSTER: We haven't committed any, yet.

MOTHER: Then why are you leaving?

LEMSTER: I want to go to my place to see what's happening.

MOTHER: You'll be killed.

LEMSTER: He might be killing Simon by mistake.

MOTHER: You're going to see that girl.

LEMSTER: I'm not.

MOTHER: We're old enough to tell each other everything. There should be no need for secrecy.

LEMSTER (to the audience): She wants me to confess I want her daughter. And yet it isn't sex. I simply want a proper human relationship. That isn't possible with her because she's too dramatic.

(He puts on his hat. MOTHER screams. He takes off his hat. Pause.)

MOTHER: I'm keeping you against your will, aren't I.

LEMSTER (to the audience): She is, but how can I tell her?

MOTHER (to the audience): He doesn't want to be rude so he's keeping quiet.

(Silence. Enter FATHER.)

FATHER (to the audience): This is Simon's place. Lemster'll be asleep by now. I can't be bothered to wake him up to kill him. He'll go back to his own place in time. I'd better go and wait for him.

(He walks off. Silence.)

MOTHER: Well, if you're going, go.

(LEMSTER puts on his hat. MOTHER screams. LEMSTER takes off his hat. Silence.)

What are you waiting for?

LEMSTER: An inspiration.

(He turns and points.)

Look! Your husband's coming through the window!

(MOTHER screams and ducks under the bed clothes. LEMSTER goes outside.)

(To the audience): Things are getting out of hand. I must move fast.)

SCENE SEVENTEEN

FATHER asleep outside the door. The GIRL sits beside the table with a tea cup on it. SIMON is near the GIRL.

SIMON: Of course communication's difficult when failure dominates, I realize that. But effort is the hallmark of the human being. You must attempt, or else you die.

(Silence.)

Well, I have every sympathy, but sympathy requires response or else it starves.

(Silence.)

You realise that you're starving me, I suppose, that language, at this moment, could help us to build a rich thing we'd never lose, a physical enjoyment so sophisticated we could ignore the pains life has to offer, including A levels.

(Silence.)

What you mean, of course, is that you've grown prudish. When you say it's no good any more you mean you're scared, and when you say you've grown out of that sort of thing you mean you want it too badly to control. Why don't you face the facts? And what'll Lemster say when he hears you haven't been to the college? I'll tell you what he'll say. He'll say he knows your sort, the witless women of the middle classes, the dough-faced mothers of the carbohydrate generation, lying like an indigestible pasta on their introverted family life, that's what he'll say.

(Silence. She pushes her tea cup towards him. He takes the cup.)

The times you've come to me begging for love. Begging for it. Well, just try begging now.

(He waits. Silence.)

You don't know what the point of living is, do you. Orgy upon orgy of tea and bread is all you want, with cocoa and a fry-up thrown in for kicks. Well, you can have it! You needn't think I'm going to waste my quickness on your corpse, my spirit on your welfare state vacuity, because I'm not! I'm going to make you one more cup of tea, and that's it.

(He goes out to the back, and then enters again immediately.)

And you needn't think I don't know what's behind it, because I do. Westminster Abbey's behind it. You've been ingested into all that Gothic, haven't you.

(LEMSTER has entered and reached the door. He now knocks.)

Oh, go to hell!

(He goes off. LEMSTER knocks again.)

FATHER (waking): Lemster!

LEMSTER: I suppose you know your wife's at Simon's place.

FATHER: But Simon's here.

LEMSTER (hollowly): Haha.

FATHER: It can't be true!

LEMSTER (to the door): Please let me in.

FATHER: And please let me in too.

LEMSTER: And what about your wife?

FATHER: I'll ring her up.

(Enter SIMON.)

SIMON: The girl next door, the nightmare life in death.

(He opens the door): Hullo.

LEMSTER (as if surprised): Good heavens. Simon!

FATHER: Why aren't you at your place with my wife?

LEMSTER (as if surprised): Your wife?

FATHER: At his place.

LEMSTER (to SIMON): Seducer! Out you go at once.

SIMON: You made this bargain.

FATHER (seeing his daughter, going in): My daughter. She comes into this somehow.

LEMSTER (following): And what's she doing here?

SIMON: You wanted to seduce her.

LEMSTER: I was out.

FATHER (to SIMON): And you were in.

SIMON (to FATHER): He went to my place to seduce her.

LEMSTER: Why did she come to my place?

SIMON: To get away from you.

LEMSTER: She thought that I was here and came for solace –

(To FATHER): as she often does when Simon's treated her badly.

SIMON: What?

FATHER: Whose bed's that?

LEMSTER: Mine.

FATHER: I've been up two nights on the trot. I think I'll close my eyes.

(He lies down.)

LEMSTER (low): You double crossed me.

SIMON (low): No.

LEMSTER (low): Then why's it all gone wrong?

SIMON (low): I've no idea.

LEMSTER (low): You want to have the girl?

SIMON: Ha!

LEMSTER: Well you can't!

SIMON: Nobody can. She's embalmed.

LEMSTER (turning to her): What? And did we like the college?

SIMON: We didn't go.

LEMSTER: What?

SIMON: No.

LEMSTER: Why?

SIMON: We had a vision.

LEMSTER: What?

FATHER (eyes closed): Her mother's worried, too. That's why she's in Simon's bed.

LEMSTER (to SIMON): How's it affected her?

SIMON: With inhibitions.

FATHER (eyes closed): Always a sign of worry, that kind of thing.

(MOTHER enters and beats on the door. She shouts before she beats.)

MOTHER: Rape! Rape! Rape! Rape!

LEMSTER: Shut up!

(Silence.)

FATHER (sitting up): Am I the only one who's tired?

LEMSTER: Go to sleep.

(FATHER lies down.)

Now look. The girl's no good to you. Buzz off.

SIMON: Oh no. She needs a quickening spirit.

LEMSTER: She needs protecting.

SIMON: Wakening.

LEMSTER: Guarding.

SIMON: Thrusting upon life.

LEMSTER: She needs a friend.

SIMON: She needs a lover.

LEMSTER: Me!

SIMON: Me!

FATHER (sitting up): How <u>can</u> I get to sleep?

SIMON: This man has just seduced your wife and now he gluttonously wants your daughter. I just want the daughter.

FATHER: Marriage?

SIMON: No.

FATHER: These days nothing's ever settled.

MOTHER: Rape!

FATHER: All right, Mother! Let her in, one of you.

LEMSTER (as if seized by invisible hands): Oh! Ah! Oh no! Let me be! Let me go!

(He collapses in the spare chair and speaks falsetto):

There was a little man and he had a little gun, right in the middle of his forehead.

FATHER: What was that?

LEMSTER (bass and falsetto): Four score and seven years ago little Miss Muffet sat on her tuffet.

(His eyes are closed in a twitching trance.)

SIMON: Snap out of it.

LEMSTER (whine): Are you there? Are you there, Caliope?

MOTHER (putting her shoulder to the door which flies open as she shouts): Rape!

(She is in.)

Behold a ruined woman!

LEMSTER (bass): Full fathom five.

MOTHER: This man has used me and then spurned me.

LEMSTER (falsetto): I have a message from Beyond.

SIMON (to the GIRL): You see the messy lives that I could take you from?

LEMSTER: A message from Beyond.

MOTHER: Simon, I've been used and spurned.

SIMON: We could go now.

MOTHER: Dear boy, don't dabble with such transient pleasures.

SIMON: A clean break, in bed, with me.

MOTHER: You need a sturdier branch to lean on.

LEMSTER (falsetto): If there's a girl in the room who's just failed her A levels she should go at once to a secretarial college in the Cromwell Road, where she will train to be a useful wife to her future husband, whose name begins with L.

SIMON: You crafty devil.

FATHER: Who would that be?

LEMSTER: L-E-M

FATHER: You! Well, that's a firmer offer than Simon's.

SIMON: You wouldn't waste –

MOTHER: Oh, Simon, let her go!

FATHER: And everything would be settled nicely.

SIMON: No!

MOTHER: Yes!

LEMSTER: It is the will of Caliope, Daughter of Time, Old as the Hills, and Young as the Bursting Shoots.

GIRL (interrupting by singing): Guide me, Oh, Thou Great Jehovah etc.

(She goes on singing until she stops to speak the last speech.)

(They all look at her.)

LEMSTER (falsetto): Silence! Silence!

(He opens his eyes. Ordinary voice): Silence!

(He shuts his eyes again.)

MOTHER: It's those Jehovah's Witnesses. You simply can't bring children into the world today.

(The GIRL gets up and goes to the back while the following conversation takes place.)

SIMON: If only all of you had let her be and never pestered her...

FATHER: Who pestered her?

MOTHER (to FATHER): Oh, you could never see the harm that you were doing.

FATHER: I never interfered.

SIMON: That's it! She'd no-one to rebel against.

MOTHER: And I had to be father, mother, brother, sister.

SIMON: Forcing her to listen to performances that...

MOTHER: Simon, if you only knew what I could teach you.

LEMSTER (who has been coming round rather elaborately): Something awful's happened.

FATHER: Has it?

LEMSTER: I can feel vibrations.

SIMON: None of you would listen when I tried to tell you.

LEMSTER: Where's she gone?

MOTHER: Ungrateful girl!

LEMSTER (rushing to the front door, which is open): She's not escaped!

SIMON: Some hope.

(Enter, singing, the GIRL dressed as a nun. She has not stopped singing the same hymn all the time she has been out.)

MOTHER: You sacrilegious baggage! Take that off!

SIMON: You fool! You should've slept with me!

LEMSTER: Pipped at the post.

FATHER: Well I never did.

GIRL (to the audience): If you reflect, you'll see this is the only conclusion I could come to. It would be painful to go over all the reasons why, but there's been little evidence that I could manage ordinary life so far. You'll remember that I'm not a great success at facing facts, although I am hardworking, I have a conscience, and I'm devoted. It's obvious this is just what I should be. There's really no need for them to make such a fuss.

(She starts singing again. At the same time the following things happen:

MOTHER has hysterics all over SIMON.

SIMON repeats his speech from the bottom of page 14,
"Her situation is the one which family units."
FATHER repeats his speech from page 18, "I'd like to
know one thing only."
LEMSTER shuts his eyes and repeats "Little Bo-Peep,"
falsetto.
The GIRL looks extremely happy.

All this at the same time.)

CURTAIN.

THE DANCERS

A pinkish mauve colour. A gramophone playing a Strauss waltz stage right. Faint noise of gaiety off.

Enter MISS PARTLIP, who is very fat, dancing with MR BOWHORN, who is very thin.

MISS PARTLIP: Oh what a strain, Mr Bowhorn!

MR BOWHORN: But what a pleasure for me, Miss Partlip.

(Enter BRIMLEY, stocky, wearing a paper hat and blowing a party whistle that extends into a paper tube.)

MR BOWHORN: Brimley's enjoying himself.

MISS PARTLIP: Oh Brimley! What a noise!

BRIMLEY: On with the motley!

(He seizes her from MR BOWHORN.)

MR BOWHORN: What? Oh! I say!

(Shrieks of glee from MISS PARTLIP. BRIMLEY is singing to the music.)

MISS PARTLIP: Oh, Mr Bowhorn!

MR BOWHORN: Careful, Brimley.

BRIMLEY: Careful, Bowhorn.

MR BOWHORN: What?

(Enter MRS FARACLOUGH laughing coarsely.)

MISS PARTLIP: Look, Mrs Faraclough!

MRS FARACLOUGH: Keep at it, Miss Partlip. Never say die!

MR BOWHORN: Will you dance, Mrs Faraclough?

MRS FARACLOUGH: No dear, I've had enough just for the moment thank you.

(She laughs. BRIMLEY, hooting, deserts MISS PARTLIP, and sweeps up MRS FARACLOUGH. Both ladies laugh and skriek. MISS PARTLIP dances with MR BOWHORN.)

MR BOWHORN: Brimley's enjoying himself!

BRIMLEY: Brimley always does!

MISS PARTLIP: He's a one, is Brimley.

MRS FARACLOUGH: You remind me of Faraclough, Brimley.

MISS PARTLIP: He reminds me of you, Mr Bowhorn, in your gayer moments.

MR BOWHORN: Really?

(MARTIN can be heard off stage, shouting "FANNY! FANNY! ")

MRS FARACLOUGH (laughing): Oh God! Let me hide!

BRIMLEY: Dance round her! Dance round her! Make a circle and dance!

MISS PARTLIP: It's only Martin.

BRIMLEY: Never mind! Dance round!

(Laughter as they all dance round MRS FARACLOUGH who kneels on the floor. Enter MARTIN pushing an armchair.)

MARTIN: Fanny!

BRIMLEY: Gone, Martin, over there!

(Laughter and gaiety from the group. MARTIN looks at them without seeing MRS FARACLOUGH, pushes his chair into a position that suits him and clambers up on it.)

MARTIN: Friends!

BRIMLEY (dancing the others on): Hooray for Martin!

MARTIN: Friends, I want to invite you all to my wedding!

(Delight from the group.)

MRS FARACLOUGH: Oh Lord.

MARTIN: Fanny?

MRS FARACLOUGH: Yes, Martin, Fanny.

(She stands up and the others dance round.)

MARTIN: What are you doing there?

MRS FARACLOUGH: Oh never mind. Get on with it now you've started.

MARTIN: I want to invite everyone to my wedding, now we're settled.

MISS PARTLIP: I love weddings. Don't you Brimley?

BRIMLEY: They bring me out in goose pimples.

MISS PARTLIP: My goodness!

MRS FARACLOUGH: Brimley's a one, Brimley is!

MR BOWHORN: Got the gift, Brimley has!

MARTIN (slightly annoyed): Who's coming to my wedding?

(Everybody stops and faces him.)

Well? Who's coming?

MRS FARACLOUGH: Everyone is, of course.

MISS PARTLIP: We know you are, Mrs Faraclough.

MRS FARACLOUGH: Turn off the music, Brimley.

BRIMLEY: At your service, Mrs Faraclough. To hear is to obey.

(He darts away to turn music off.)

MRS FARACLOUGH (going to the chair): Now then, Martin, shift over.

MARTIN: There's not room for both of us.

MRS FARACLOUGH (beginning to climb up): We'll see about that. Ooops!

MISS PARTLIP: Oooh! The springs! I'm always worried about the springs.

BRIMLEY: One of your hazards, is it, Miss Partlip?

MR BOWHORN: Now, now, Brimley.

MISS PARTLIP: He's quite right. It is.

MARTIN: Fanny, there's not room for us both. Please get down.

MRS FARACLOUGH: You'll find something bigger than this, before our wedding.

(Winks at MR BOWHORN): Eh, Mr Bowhorn?

MISS PARTLIP: Oh!

MR BOWHORN (laughing): I don't know, Mrs Faraclough!

MARTIN: Don't make jokes at the expense of my furniture.

MRS FARACLOUGH (giving up the climb): Go and get your other armchair, then, there's a love.

BRIMLEY: I'll get the other armchair.

(BRIMLEY darts away, blowing his party whistle.)

MARTIN (calling): You needn't bother! I'm going to make

my speech from here, alone.

MISS PARTLIP: You ought to wait for Brimley to come back, Martin.

MRS FARACLOUGH: Then I can stand beside you to blush at the right places.

MARTIN: There'll be no need to blush. I'm not going to be coarse.

MR BOWHORN: Well said, Martin.

MRS FARACLOUGH: But you're going to be coarse later aren't you? You aren't going to let me down just because you've got good manners?

MISS PARTLIP: I hope this works out all right.

MRS FARACLOUGH: You hope? Martin?

MARTIN: The word coarse is limiting.

MRS FARACLOUGH: Limiting! (Pause, smile): Oh! (She laughs): My God, then, we're in for a bit of a pounding, aren't we? (She laughs.)

MISS PARTLIP: Oh!

MR BOWHORN: Brimley! Hurry up, man.

MRS FARACLOUGH (laughing): I'll match you, Martin, don't you worry! Bounce for bounce, tit for tat! (Laughs.)

MARTIN (surprised): Brimley!

(MRS FARACLOUGH laughs on. The others all call for BRIMLEY, with a great hooting. BRIMLEY enters pushing the matching armchair.)

BRIMLEY: Masters, I come.

MRS FARACLOUGH (stopping): There's a good boy, Brimley. Fetch it here.

BRIMLEY: My business is to serve and my pleasure is my business.

(MRS FARACLOUGH laughs and nudges him.)

MISS PARTLIP: Do hurry up, Mrs Faraclough, and show us how you look up there beside him.

MRS FARACLOUGH: We're not going to show you much, Miss Partlip, I can tell you.

MISS PARTLIP: What do you mean?

MARTIN: Ladies and gentlemen!

MRS FARACLOUGH: Oops!

(She clambers on to the second armchair as MARTIN speaks.)

MARTIN: The lovely widow Faraclough and I are to be married, as is public knowledge. We want our friends and neighbours and all who love us and wish us well to come to our wedding and enjoy with us the sweet sadness of the celebrations.

MRS FARACLOUGH: Sadness?

MISS PARTLIP: Of course.

MARTIN: Certainly, Fanny. I suppose if you haven't been to as many weddings as I have, you won't know how they serve to fuse the great diversity of human feelings. Although we rejoice at them because they are a witness to true love, we also weep at them because the change they bring is sad. Only if you have the mind of a revolutionary can you look ahead to all the altered circumstances the newly weds must face and not cry out with pain at the vision.

BRIMLEY: From tea time onwards everything is different in marriage.

MR BOWHORN (warningly): Brimley.

MARTIN: For us poor mortals, however, it isn't possible to look ahead and see what's happening out there. Those who can are rarely happy men. Jeremiah, for example. Ruskin. We simple folk do not see, and we are happy, happy even though we have to live through what the others have foretold. Even in the bleakest, blackest days when everything has happened as Matthew Arnold said ...

MISS PARTLIP: Matthew Arnold! Well!

MARTIN: Even in these hellish days we are happy. For not only can we not see into the future. We can see neither into the present, and only obscurely into the past.

BRIMLEY: Bravo!

MR BOWHORN: Well said, sir, well said.

MARTIN: Ignorance, therefore, is bliss. But, friends, think of God.

(Everyone looks pious, except MRS FARACLOUGH, who looks amazed.)

He knows what's going on in the future. He feels it, is it, will be it, and when the time comes, was it. What agony is there for God in all that.

(Solemn pause.)

A revolutionary, now, can absorb such pain, can march forward, smiling and say "Experience! How very exciting to be alive!" But everyone knows that God and His prophets are not revolutionaries. They are conservative by nature and reformist by conscience, and they suffer exceedingly accordingly.

MR BOWHORN: True, true.

BRIMLEY: Very true.

MARTIN: What was I talking about to start with?

MRS FARACLOUGH: Yes. I wondered when you'd come back to that. Our wedding, Martin, was what you were talking about. You were going to invite everyone to come to it.

MARTIN: Oh yes.

MRS FARACLOUGH: But I can't say you made it sound a riotous feast of joy unbounded.

MARTIN: Well ...

MRS FARACLOUGH: In fact, I don't know whether I'll come to it unless it shows signs of picking up and bedding down with a great deal more zest than you've shown yourself prepared for.

MARTIN: I haven't said anything about our actual marriage, Fanny ...

MRS FARACLOUGH: No, and I dread to think what you will say when you do.

MARTIN (cross): I shan't say anything! Marriage is sacred!

MRS FARACLOUGH: Marriage is fun!

MARTIN: Well yes, that's what I mean.

MRS FARACLOUGH: Now listen here, Martin, Faraclough may have had a weak heart, but he was a trier, by God, and you'd never find him giving in and talking, no matter what went wrong.

MARTIN: Went wrong?

MRS FARACLOUGH: He kept on, Faraclough did, until his heart gave out, and never once in fifteen years did he stop to preach a sermon.

MARTIN: Well, nor shall I! I've never preached a sermon in my life! You never heard me preach a sermon, Mr Bowhorn.

MR BOWHORN: Never, Martin.

MRS FARACLOUGH: You may have caught the taste for it now you've started.

BRIMLEY: True.

MR BOWHORN: Shut up.

MARTIN: I haven't started!

MRS FARACLOUGH: What was that, then, about God?

MARTIN: That was just a reference!

MRS FARACLOUGH: First a reference, then a sermon, who knows where you'll stop!

MARTIN (very cross): I was following a truth the conversation threw up!

MRS FARACLOUGH: That's it!

(She climbs down.)

I want a man who talks less and laughs more!

BRIMLEY (jumping forward): Aha!

MRS FARACLOUGH (laughing): Oho!

BRIMLEY: Some music, Mrs F.?

MARTIN: Fanny!

MRS FARACLOUGH: Brisk, Brimley.

BRIMLEY: As you wish, Mrs F.

(He darts away to the record player.)

MISS PARTLIP (clambering onto the vacated chair): Now, Martin, don't be discouraged by this little upset.

MARTIN: I'm not discouraged. Why should I be?

MISS PARTLIP: Well, you could be.

MARTIN: Well, I'm not.

MISS PARTLIP: Well, good.

MRS FARACLOUGH: Something sprightly, Brimley.

BRIMLEY: With a jig in it!

MRS FARACLOUGH: With a jig in it!

(She roars with laughter. Can-Can music plays out. BRIMLEY and MRS FARACLOUGH dance away. MR BOWHORN watches them. MISS PARTLIP totters in the chair and reaches out to grasp the hand of MARTIN, who looks preoccupied. She begins patting his hand. BRIMLEY blows his whistle.)

MRS FARACLOUGH: Oh Brimley! You do such mystical, obvious things to me!

(He whirls her off the stage. MR BOWHORN watches, then turns to MARTIN, then turns off music. The light begins to change.)

MISS PARTLIP (still patting and continuing as she has been doing since she started patting): There, there there, there, there, there, there, there, there.

MARTIN: Stop, Miss Partlip.

MISS PARTLIP (continuing): There, there, there, etc.

MARTIN: Stop! Please!

(He tugs his hand away. MISS PARTLIP totters. MR BOWHORN, who has sat on the arm of her chair, balances her.)

MR BOWHORN: Steady!

(MISS PARTLIP steadies herself.)

MISS PARTLIP: It is one of the gifts of the larger lady that she can keep her balance more easily than those of slighter build.

MR BOWHORN: I bow to you, madame.

MISS PARTLIP: Thank you.

(The light by now is a pretty pale blue.)

MISS PARTLIP (fanning herself): Well! I haven't climbed so far for years!

MR BOWHORN: You're quite the athlete, Miss Partlip.

MISS PARTLIP: The fuller figure is noted also for swimming, as you probably know.

MARTIN: It floats easily.

MISS PARTLIP: No, Martin, it swims easily. It's built that way.

MR BOWHORN: Fish-like, as it were.

MARTIN: I don't see much point in standing on this chair any longer.

MISS PARTLIP: Oh!

MARTIN: What?

MISS PARTLIP: I came up here to comfort you, Martin.

MARTIN: Can't you do it on the floor?

MISS PARTLIP: It's just that it cost me something to get here.

MARTIN: Oh. I've been thoughtless.

MISS PARTLIP: Oh no! Please don't stay up here on my account.

MARTIN: I find it very pleasant up here, if a little insecure. (Gloomy): But then insecurity is the spice of life.

MISS PARTLIP: Well ... anyway ... you must try and not let this upset you, Martin.

MARTIN (gloomy): It's a slight misunderstanding brought on by ecstasy at the thought of marriage.

MISS PARTLIP: I think perhaps we will go down after all. Um ... Mr Bowhorn, would there be a stool or something?

MR BOWHORN: I'll see what I can find.

MISS PARTLIP: I am so grateful.

MR BOWHORN: Not at all.

(He goes out.)

MISS PARTLIP: Now we can have a little talk.

MARTIN (gloomy): Oh.

MISS PARTLIP: You were throwing yourself away, you know.

MARTIN (gloomy silence.)

MISS PARTLIP: A man like you, Martin, needs routine as a background to his activities.

(Pause.)

MARTIN (gloomily): You're referring to yourself, Miss Partlip.

MISS PARTLIP: Routine is all I've been able to manage.

MARTIN: I'm afraid marriage to you would be ...

(Pause. MARTIN looks awkward.)

.... obscene.

(MISS PARTLIP looks at him and nearly cries. MARTIN shifts uneasily. MISS PARTLIP controls herself.)

MISS PARTLIP: Because I'm fat?

MARTIN (anguished): We can't help these things.

MISS PARTLIP (near tears): No.

(Pause.)

I wish Mr Bowhorn hadn't gone away.

(Pause.)

But he's so kind.

(Pause.)

He makes me feel so humble.

MARTIN: He can afford to.

MISS PARTLIP: I think that's less than generous.

MARTIN: I apologise.

MISS PARTLIP: He's a great man in his way.

MARTIN: Exactly. If a great man can't make you feel humble, a humble one can't.

MISS PARTLIP (very near tears): Martin, you must try not to be clever.

MARTIN (anguished): I do try. I apologise.

MISS PARTLIP (near tears): Mr Bowhorn has, after all, gone to get a stool.

MARTIN: It'll be interesting to see if he finds one.

MISS PARTLIP (near tears): The intention is what we must judge, Martin.

MARTIN (cynical): Exactly.

MISS PARTLIP (near tears): Martin?

MARTIN (anguished): You see the best in everything, Miss Partlip and I am humbled. I do, I do apologise.

(Enter MR BOWHORN with a stool.)

MR BOWHORN: Here we are.

MISS PARTLIP: There! You see?

MR BOWHORN: Your stool, dear lady.

MISS PARTLIP: Thank you.

MR BOWHORN: Allow me.

MISS PARTLIP: Thank you.

(She comes down.)

May I sit in your chair, Martin?

MARTIN: Do.

(He comes down and stands about.)

MISS PARTLIP: You're sure?

MARTIN (snappily): Of course I'm sure.

MISS PARTLIP (near tears): Thank you.

(She sits.)

MR BOWHORN (tactfully): I'll put on some quiet music.

(MARTIN fidgets. MR BOWHORN puts on the second movement of Bach's concerto for two violins. MR BOWHORN turns his back and hums to himself. MISS PARTLIP watches.)

MISS PARTLIP (nostalgically): The slighter figure.

(Pause.)

Do you have longings for your childhood?

MARTIN: Sometimes.

MISS PARTLIP: I lived in Folkestone. Everyone used to say what a cheery girl I was.

MARTIN: Were you slim, then?

MISS PARTLIP: No. But no-one ever referred to it.

MARTIN: Perhaps they should have. Truth is always useful.

(MISS PARTLIP cries quietly. Silence, except for this and music. MARTIN finds it all too much and quickly turns off the record.)

MISS PARTLIP (quietly regaining control of herself): I'm very sorry, Martin.

MARTIN (anguished, then): When you've finished with the chairs I'd like them back. They're all I've managed to collect so far.

(He goes out. MISS PARTLIP cries.)

MR BOWHORN: Now, now, now.

(Pause.)

You haven't lost a lot with Martin, you know.

(MISS PARTLIP dries her eyes gradually.)

He's a pretty ordinary little man.

MISS PARTLIP: He was tasteful.

MR BOWHORN: Sort of crept into it, though, if you know what I mean. He wasn't able to assume anything. Do you smoke, Elizabeth?

(MISS PARTLIP shakes her head, and the light begins to turn royal purple.)

You don't mind if I do? I'm the only person of us all who smokes.

MISS PARTLIP: No-one's ever suggested that the rest of us might, have they.

MR BOWHORN: I always think it's unhealthy.

MISS PARTLIP: Martin smokes a pipe, but he finds it rather comic.

MR BOWHORN: Martin's cynicism springs from want of ease.

(He is smoking.)

Now Martin could never smoke a cigarette. He's not the type.

MISS PARTLIP: The smoke always went in my eyes when I tried. (Near tears): My piggy little eyes.

MR BOWHORN (becoming grand: the lights have now completely changed to royal purple): Miss Partlip. You could pronounce your name Parlp, couldn't you, or Plip. Or Parlip. Or Partly. Or Parley. Parley's interesting, because you could be of French descent, especially coming from Folkestone. Partlip was probably an anglicisation of Porte Loupe, referring to the family coat of arms, which incorporated a wolf being carried aloft by a huntsman, deriving from a tale of your ancestors, who hunted the wolves out of Normandy. Like Bowhorn.

MISS PARTLIP (surprised): Bowhorn?

MR BOWHORN: Normally, the family intimates pronounce it Bowen, an aristocratic English name if ever there was one. Really, though, it's Bourne. The Bourne from which no traveller returns, you know.

MISS PARTLIP: Really?

MR BOWHORN: And Pangbourne, Eastbourne, Sittingbourne, Bournemouth. The family has enriched our island heritage from the coffers of its name.

MISS PARTLIP: The Partlips were simple farmers.

MR BOWHORN: In the squirearchy, though. There's no doubt we might make a match of it, Elizabeth.

MISS PARTLIP: Don't joke, Mr Bowhorn.

MR BOWHORN: I'm not joking.

MISS PARTLIP: Will you be more explicit?

MR BOWHORN: I'm stating a fact, that we might, with our various pedigrees, make a married couple worthy of respect. Mr and Mrs Edward Parley-Bourne.

MISS PARTLIP: Nonsense.

MR BOWHORN: Edward Parley-Bourne, Bart, Viscount Parley-Bourne of Bourne, Duke of Bournemouth.

(Pause.)

MISS PARTLIP: Do sit down Edward if we're going to talk any further.

(MR BOWHORN laughs in a dignified way as if trying it out.)

It would be nice to get something settled, what with Martin's trouble and everything.

MR BOWHORN: Do you really think I'm going to sit in one of those chairs?

MISS PARTLIP: It would be a gracious thing to do.

MR BOWHORN: Ah. Gracious. Shall I bestow myself on these chairs for a charitable few minutes then?

MISS PARTLIP: Yes.

(He sits grandly.)

There's no denying it, you of the slighter figure are able to adapt yourselves in a way we ampler folk are not.

(MR BOWHORN smiles.)

Martin was probably right. I wouldn't be a pretty sight in bed.

MR BOWHORN (nervous): I don't think I'm ready for that kind of conversation yet.

MISS PARTLIP: Edward, we're more or less old friends. We should be frank. Besides, frankness is rather pleasant in a salty kind of way. I like saying words like contraceptive every now and then.

MR BOWHORN (loudly): How do I put this cigarette out?

MISS PARTLIP: Don't you?

MR BOWHORN: No.

MISS PARTLIP: It fills me with a kind of terror, like whisky, and then it settles in and it leaves a tang.

(She savours the moment.)

MR BOWHORN: You aren't going to say it again?

MISS PARTLIP: No.

MR BOWHORN: Then how can I put this cigarette out?

MISS PARTLIP: Tread on it.

(MR BOWHORN laughs and does so.)

Very neat.

MR BOWHORN (rising grandly): Elizabeth, the union of our two houses is a consummation which I, the last of the Bournes, feel I must bend my mind to with all despatch. I am therefore going to propose to you. But before I do I want to know if you're likely to accept.

MISS PARTLIP: No, Edward, I could only offer routine. I haven't got your flourish.

MR BOWHORN: Then I may definitely expect a rejection?

MISS PARTLIP: Yes.

MR BOWHORN: Very well.

(He goes to the record player. He puts on grand march from Aida. He approaches, bows, nips back to turn off the record player, returns to bowing position, stands up.)

Madame, I am a man of solitude. For years I have tried to serve my country and my God with all the strength at my command, with all my soul, with all my mind, with all ... everything. Now I have reached the autumn, and winter, to coin a phrase, is hard behind. I find I cannot traverse the final passage in the corridors terrestrial alone. I need the society of a trusted friend.

MISS PARTLIP: A trusted friend?

MR BOWHORN: A trusted friend, Miss Partlip, I bow to you and with humility request that you yield your home to share my hoary days, and be the trusted friend of whom I speak.

MISS PARTLIP: Could you go into it a little further?

MR BOWHORN: Into what?

MISS PARTLIP: The trusted friend.

MR BOWHORN: If ... yes, certainly. The one I wish to make my own will be my trusted friend, the fireside companion, one of the old folks at home. We'll rule together from our bungalow in ancient order and sweet mellowness.

MISS PARTLIP: The kiss of the sun for pardon,
              The song of the birds for mirth,

TOGETHER: You are nearer God's heart in a garden,
              Than anywhere else on earth.

(Silence.)

MISS PARTLIP: Yes. I think I'll accept you, Edward.

MR BOWHORN: What?

MISS PARTLIP: But no funny names.

MR BOWHORN: What d'you mean, you'll accept?

MISS PARTLIP: I've changed my mind.

MR BOWHORN (terrified): No!

MISS PARTLIP: Why not?

MR BOWHORN: I'd never have asked you if I'd thought you were going to accept!

MISS PARTLIP: Oh!

MR BOWHORN: I only wanted to propose! I don't want a wife!

MISS PARTLIP (near tears): Edward!

(Coarse laughter off from MRS FARACLOUGH.)

MR BOWHORN: Exposed! And before that woman!

MISS PARTLIP: No, Edward. You can trust me. I won't reveal your secret.

MR BOWHORN: Eh?

MISS PARTLIP: My lips are sealed.

MR BOWHORN: Oh dear, oh dear, oh dear! I don't remember having hurt myself so badly in my life.

(Enter MRS FARACLOUGH, laughing, in disarray.)

MRS FARACLOUGH: Oh, Brimley's all hands, Brimley is! A right roisterer!

MR BOWHORN: My God! Some people!

MRS FARACLOUGH: Oh, being a bit Holy, are we?

MR BOWHORN: No.

MRS FARACLOUGH: Saint Edward Le Bowhorn.

MR BOWHORN: What?

MISS PARTLIP (laughs.)

MR BOWHORN: What's wrong with that?

MISS PARTLIP: Nothing! I'm sure you'll find a use for it!

MR BOWHORN: Le Beau Homme. Sainte Edouard Le Beau Homme, burned at the stake before Notre Dame Cathedral.

(He smiles and turns away with a saintly expression and clasped hands.)

MRS FARACLOUGH (sitting): Well, everything's a bit upset, isn't it?

MISS PARTLIP: Yes.

MRS FARACLOUGH: These chairs are still mine, you know.

Part of the dowry.

MISS PARTLIP: You're still engaged?

MRS FARACLOUGH: Certainly.

MISS PARTLIP: Then if you don't mind, I'll stand up. I don't want to sit in your chairs.

MRS FARACLOUGH: Suit yourself.

(MISS PARTLIP struggles to get up.)

MR BOWHORN: Sainte Edouard Le Beau Homme was a handsome creature, and a virgin. He was persecuted by the nuns of Paris in twelve hundred and something, and died blessing his tormentors from the stake. He is usually portrayed as an abstracted figure moving with grace through the stews of Paris and never displaying a moment's weakness. A serene man. Edouard Le Tranquil.

MISS PARTLIP (struggling): If I could just get out of here ..

(MRS FARACLOUGH leans over, and thrusts her hand behind MISS PARTLIP's bottom.)

(Leaping free): Oh!

(MRS FARACLOUGH laughs.)

I told Martin he was well rid of you and my goodness I was right!

(MRS FARACLOUGH blows a raspberry.)

MISS PARTLIP: Mr Bowhorn, I turn to you, despite our awkwardness ...

MR BOWHORN: Dear child, your sins are forgiven you. Just put on the next record.

MISS PARTLIP: But ...

MR BOWHORN: Just do as I say, dear child.

MISS PARTLIP: But ...

MR BOWHORN: Do as I say!

(She goes to the record player.)

MRS FARACLOUGH: Prigs.

MR BOWHORN: Those that have eyes to see, let them see.

MRS FARACLOUGH: As a matter of fact you two might be rather well suited. Have you ever thought about it?

(MISS PARTLIP quickly puts on a record of a Gregorian

chant, while MR BOWHORN falls hurriedly to his knees.)

MR BOWHORN (in a loud voice and hurriedly): Forgive them their sins oh Lord for they know not what they do!

MRS FARACLOUGH: What does he mean?

MISS PARTLIP: If the cap fits.

MRS FARACLOUGH: Does he mean me?

MR BOWHORN (as above): The lusts of the flesh are strong but the lusts of the spirit are stronger!

MRS FARACLOUGH (getting up): The old devil!

MR BOWHORN: Blessed are the pure in heart for they shall see God!

MRS FARACLOUGH: There's lots more to see before that, Edward Bowhorn, as well you know! Now then!

(She jumps on him and starts to undress him.)

MR BOWHORN: Thou shalt not commit fornication! Thou shalt not commit fornication! Thou shalt not commit fornication! Turn the record louder! Turn the record louder! Turn the record louder!

(MISS PARTLIP does so. It drowns most of the noise, though parts of the general confession can be heard coming through from MR BOWHORN. MISS PARTLIP, after looking on unmoved becomes startled. She turns off the record. MR BOWHORN has minor clothes missing.)

MR BOWHORN (sitting up): Dear me.

MRS FARACLOUGH: I can't abide hypocrisy.

MR BOWHORN: I apologise.

MRS FARACLOUGH: Granted.

MISS PARTLIP: I thought the whole interlude was disgusting. I'm surprised at you Mr Bowhorn. You were enjoying it.

(MR BOWHORN crawls to retrieve his clothes and puts them on.)

MR BOWHORN: Put on some more music, Miss Partlip.

MRS FARACLOUGH: None But The Lonely Heart.

(She giggles.)

MISS PARTLIP: That's my favourite record, and I'm not going to associate it with all this unpleasantness.

MR BOWHORN: Anything, dear lady, but do oblige us poor sinners with something.

(MISS PARTLIP puts on a record. MRS FARACLOUGH and MR BOWHORN are still on the floor. The record is a Victor Sylvester foxtrot. All look rather dissatisfied.)

MRS FARACLOUGH: The posher you get, the less body there is.

MISS PARTLIP: At least it's reducing the temperature.

(The light is turning very pale. Pause.)

MRS FARACLOUGH: Martin's up to something.

MR BOWHORN: Unreliable lad, I'm afraid.

MISS PARTLIP: All of us are unreliable in some ways.

(MR BOWHORN looks unhappy.)

MRS FARACLOUGH: There are ways and ways.

(MR BOWHORN stills looks unhappy.)

Well, since there's no-one else, Mr Bowhorn, will you dance?

MR BOWHORN: Delighted.

(They get up and dance. They dance very neatly while MISS PARTLIP kicks the stool, and then, in remorse, sits on it.)

MRS FARACLOUGH: I left Brimley asleep.

MR BOWHORN: A strange man, Brimley.

MRS FARACLOUGH: A trier, though. A real trier.

MR BOWHORN: Irresponsible.

MRS FARACLOUGH: You're all right, in a flannel bagsy kind of way, aren't you.

MR BOWHORN: I used to enjoy the thé dansant as a lad. Very relaxing I used to find it.

MRS FARACLOUGH: I should've thought you and Miss Partlip had a lot in common.

MR BOWHORN: There's always the psychological as well as the sociological, you know. She's closer to her background than I am.

MRS FARACLOUGH (to MISS PARTLIP): You all right, dear?

MISS PARTLIP: Yes thank you.

MRS FARACLOUGH: Still worried about the chairs, are you?

MISS PARTLIP (unable to reply.)

MRS FARACLOUGH: Will you manage on that stool, all of you?

MR BOWHORN: Now, Mrs Faraclough, is that generous?

MRS FARACLOUGH: No.

MISS PARTLIP: Don't let me interrupt you.

MRS FARACLOUGH: No, dear.

MISS PARTLIP: Carry on with your hanky-panky, and your footy-footy, and your petting, and all that.

MRS FARACLOUGH: Everyone's jealous of a widow, you know. She's had so much it's not fair she should have any more.

MR BOWHORN: It must be very hard for you.

MRS FARACLOUGH: It is, really.

MR BOWHORN: I shall always give you my support in your troubles.

MR PARTLIP: Just go on as if I weren't here.

MRS FARACLOUGH: Not easy, dear, with your figure, but we'll try.

MISS PARTLIP (standing up): I've had enough!

(The others go on dancing.)

Mr Bowhorn, are you going to let her call me fat?

(The others stop dancing.)

MR BOWHORN: Difficult to stop her when you are fat.

MISS PARTLIP: There's no need to let her insult me publicly!

MR BOWHORN: Well, if you consider fatness insulting ...

MISS PARTLIP: The fuller figure is capable of great dignity, and should never be mocked.

MRS FARACLOUGH: Turn off the record.

(MR BOWHORN obeys.)

Now. The fuller figure means fat, flabby, uncooked

lard, held in by corsets and stays and great lumps of machinery. You are a fat and disgusting woman.

MR BOWHORN: Oh I say!

MISS PARTLIP: Let her go on.

MRS FARACLOUGH: I'm not going on. I'm telling you straight that you're fat. There's nothing more to it.

MR BOWHORN: She can't help it, you know.

MRS FARACLOUGH: Oh no, she can't help it, and it's made her what she is, a prissy old bag.

MR BOWHORN: Now, now, Mrs Faraclough, we can't have this.

MISS PARTLIP: Let her go on.

MRS FARACLOUGH: I'm not going on! I've told you! You're fat, mountainously fat! You're not simply the fuller figure, you're fat!

(Pause. The lights begin to change to orange.)

MISS PARTLIP: Have you finished?

MRS FARACLOUGH: Finished? I should say I've finished, you great fat thing!

MISS PARTLIP: You haven't finished.

MRS FARACLOUGH: Yes I have, I've finished! You're fat, and that's it!

MISS PARTLIP: Well, now, so I'm fat. And you're coarse.

MRS FARACLOUGH: Yes, coarse and proud of it!

MISS PARTLIP: Nasty smutty woman.

MRS FARACLOUGH: Smutty?

MISS PARTLIP: Like a fox, rolling in it's own dirt.

MRS FARACLOUGH: My God, you ignorant, ignorant old cow!

MISS PARTLIP: A very rude, nasty woman with a smutty little mind.

MRS FARACLOUGH (unbelieving, angry and impotent): You don't know smut from coarseness, do you? You don't know anything about anything, do you? Just because I have a bit of fun ... smutty! Oh God, you just don't know, do you, you bloody ignorant, old, fat woman!

MR BOWHORN: Now, now.

MRS FARACLOUGH: But she doesn't know! I'm coarse!
I'm proud of being coarse! I've never done anything
smutty in my life!

MISS PARTLIP: I said you were smutty and I meant it.

MRS FARACLOUGH (fuming and about to leap forward):
You!

MR BOWHORN: Now then please! Music hath charms to
soothe the savage beast.

MISS PARTLIP: Breast.

MR BOWHORN: Beast or breast, it doesn't matter.

(He puts on a record which turns out to be Die Walküre.
All react variously. Hurriedly MR BOWHORN takes it
off and puts on The Trout. The lights remain orange.)

There. Civilised behaviour is expected of us now.

(Silence.)

MISS PARTLIP (seated on her stool): What d'you mean,
Martin's up to something?

(Pause.)

I'm speaking to you. What d'you mean, Martin's up to
something?

MRS FARACLOUGH (sulking): Fancy dress or something, I
don't know.

MISS PARTLIP: That doesn't sound like Martin.

MRS FARACLOUGH: I tell you, he's up to something.

MR BOWHORN: His chairs are really quite ridiculous.

(He goes over to look at them.)

MRS FARACLOUGH: There's nothing wrong with them.

MR BOWHORN: Try arranging them.

MRS FARACLOUGH: Arranging them?

MR BOWHORN (pushing them about): They don't go with
anything.

MRS FARACLOUGH: They're a bit shabby, that's all.

MR BOWHORN: Like Martin.

MISS PARTLIP: Mr Bowhorn, let us be civilised.

(They sit.)

MR BOWHORN: Martin is shabby, that's all there is to say.

MRS FARACLOUGH: I wonder if that's why he's trying on his funny clothes?

MR BOWHORN: A nasty shabby little man.

(MISS PARTLIP gets up and takes off the record. Then she sits.)

MISS PARTLIP: It's nice when we're quiet.

MR BOWHORN: I think Martin's mad.

MRS FARACLOUGH (restless): For goodness sake!

MR BOWHORN: What would you say to me as a husband?

MRS FARACLOUGH: You? (She laughs): Too stringy. Not enough core.

(MISS PARTLIP laughs.)

What's funny, then?

MISS PARTLIP: Oh, nothing.

MRS FARACLOUGH (nervous and irritated): Then don't laugh!

MR BOWHORN: I can't help being stringy, you know. In fact I've always held that one should be what one is to the full, and that's the sort of person I am constantly on the look out for. I should say, for example, that you, Miss Partlip, were a great spiritual success, by being as fat as you can possibly be, and I, in my modest way, am another, by being stringy. The Bournes were always cadaverous, though of course, immaculate.

MRS FARACLOUGH: You run on, don't you?

MISS PARTLIP: Conversation is a dying art.

MR BOWHORN: Indeed, Miss Partlip. Quite right.

MRS FARACLOUGH: So what about Martin? He isn't anything much.

MR BOWHORN: Yes.

MRS FARACLOUGH: Yes what?

MR BOWHORN: Martin's an utter failure.

MRS FARACLOUGH: Oh!

MR BOWHORN: And you, being so coarse, are a success.

MRS FARACLOUGH: And Miss Partlip, being fat.

MISS PARTLIP: And Mr Bowhorn, being stringy.

MRS FARACLOUGH: Well! What a surprise!

(Pause. MRS FARACLOUGH and MR BOWHORN peer at one another and smile. They glance at MISS PARTLIP who smiles. They bring their chairs to the middle of the stage. MISS PARTLIP brings her stool. They all face the audience.)

MR BOWHORN: He needs to be dispensed with, really. He comes between us.

MISS PARTLIP: Education could do a lot for him.

MRS FARACLOUGH (scornful): What sort of education?

MR BOWHORN: Quite right, Mrs Faraclough. He needs to see the seamy side of life.

MRS FARACLOUGH: My side.

MISS PARTLIP: Your side isn't the only side.

MR BOWHORN: He needs to be brought out, Elizabeth.

MRS FARACLOUGH: He's a late developer.

MR BOWHORN: In many ways he's still a child.

MISS PARTLIP: I suppose he needs to have one of those brutal experiences that mature a man so well.

MRS FARACLOUGH: Like me.

MISS PARTLIP: The army used to be very good.

MR BOWHORN: He'd miss the point.

MISS PARTLIP: The Salvation Army then.

MRS FARACLOUGH: The Salvation Army? They won't teach Martin anything! You haven't the faintest idea, have you?

MR BOWHORN (leaping up nervously): Music!

MRS FARACLOUGH: Oh God.

(The Wagner piece plays again. Various reactions. MR BOWHORN takes it off hurriedly.)

MR BOWHORN: How many records of that are there?

(He replaces it with Holst's Jupiter. The colour glows

angrier and angrier.)

There. (He remains standing): Martin needs to work with men. On the shop floor with men. Down the mines with men. Confronting death with men. A man can only command when he has learnt to obey. We must help to keep him straight and cure his originality ...

MISS PARTLIP: Martin's not original.

MR BOWHORN: What?

MISS PARTLIP (going to record player and taking the record off): He 's a very thoughtful person, and it would be a great sadness if he lost that thoughtfulness for others which characterises him at his best.

(Violin solo of None But The Lonely Heart.)

He should always have that personal fondness for people that everyone admired so much in my brother, lost at sea off the coast of Newfoundland. He needs to understand that it's the little things of life that matter.

MR BOWHORN (irritated, and taking off the record): He needs to be a stalwart fellow, that's what he needs to be!

MARTIN (off): I shall be coming shortly! Are you going to be ready?

MR BOWHORN (to the others): And are we? No, we're not. We're frittering away our time. We need an inspired suggestion.

MRS FARACLOUGH: Brothel keeper.

MISS PARTLIP: Never!

MR BOWHORN: Able seaman.

MISS PARTLIP: Youth leader!

MRS FARACLOUGH: God.

MR BOWHORN: All of them!

MRS FARACLOUGH: One after the other?

MR BOWHORN: Beginning with - your idea.

MISS PARTLIP: And ending triumphantly with mine!

MRS FARACLOUGH: You really want to suffocate him, don't you?

MR BOWHORN: But it is a logical order. Two spells in the

ranks and a commission at the end.

MARTIN (off): Put on some music, will you?

MISS PARTLIP: Yes, Martin.

(She goes to the record player.)

MARTIN (off): And clear my chairs out of the way.

MR BOWHORN (moving them): But we haven't decided!

MISS PARTLIP: Yes we have. The stool, Fanny.

(MRS FARACLOUGH picks it up and removes it. MRS FARACLOUGH is about to speak and is drowned by None But The Lonely Heart.)

MARTIN (off, very loudly): No, Miss Partlip.

(MISS PARTLIP takes it off.)

MRS FARACLOUGH (helping to push the chairs back): I want him to decide things for himself.

(MISS PARTLIP has put on a well known Gilbert and Sullivan chorus.)

MARTIN: No!

(It goes on.)

No!!!

MISS PARTLIP (taking it off): You're very difficult.

MR BOWHORN: Should we try talking to him?

MRS FARACLOUGH: What about, for Heaven's sake?

MR BOWHORN: His character.

MRS FARACLOUGH: No. We've got to pitch him into life.

MARTIN: Hurry up!

MISS PARTLIP: I'll talk to him.

MRS FARACLOUGH: If there's any talking to be done, I'll do it.

MR BOWHORN: I don't want to pull rank in any way ...

MARTIN (off, with authority): Oh for goodness sake hurry up out there!

(Silence.)

MR BOWHORN: We'll play it by ear. What do you say, Mrs Faraclough?

MRS FARACLOUGH (snorts.)

MISS PARTLIP: You know my views.

MARTIN (with strained patience, off): Miss Partlip, please put on the record you have in your hand, and let's hear it.

(MISS PARTLIP does so. It is the Wagner again. Various reactions. Scene very red. MISS PARTLIP moves to remove record.)

MARTIN (enormous voice): Right! Stand back every one!

(Enter MARTIN in a huge, magnificent dress. It should dwarf everyone, and involve buskins. He can be seen in the middle of it.

MARTIN carries off this entry superbly and everyone is stunned. Having arrived, MARTIN indicates to MISS PARTLIP to turn off the sound. She does.)

MR BOWHORN (finding his voice): Well, well, well, eh, Martin? Well! I must say! Well!

(Silence. MARTIN is obviously difficult to approach, as someone tries it and does not succeed.)

Aura, I think the word is, Martin. Quite an aura. Yes.

MARTIN: Brimley: Brimley's not here, I see.

(All look around uncomfortably.)

MRS FARACLOUGH: I think he's asleep.

MARTIN: Oh yes?

MRS FARACLOUGH: I'm afraid so.

MR BOWHORN: Shall we wake him up.

MARTIN: Oh no.

(The colour begins to soften.)

Now, Fanny, where are our chairs?

MRS FARACLOUGH: Over there.

MARTIN: Looking after them, are you, Fanny?

MRS FARACLOUGH: Yes, Martin.

MARTIN: And Miss Partlip? Where's your Edward?

MR BOWHORN: What? Oh!

MISS PARTLIP: After all!

MR BOWHORN: So it seems.

(They come together.)

MARTIN: How nice. You all give me such very great joy. Fanny, I believe you used to fear that marriage to me might lead to oratory.

MRS FARACLOUGH: Yes, Martin.

MARTIN: It might well do that, Fanny. I find I have the gift. Please put on a gramophone record.

(MRS FARACLOUGH goes to the record player.)

All this pleases me more than I can ever remember being pleased before. Are you all happy?

ALL: Yes, Martin.

MARTIN: And are you ready, Fanny?

MRS FARACLOUGH: Yes, Martin.

MARTIN: Then when I give the word, let us all dance, cheerfully. Fanny? Now.

(Dance Of The Flowers. MISS PARTLIP and MR BOWHORN begin to dance round each other and round MARTIN. MRS FARACLOUGH closer to him, also begins to dance round him. After a second or two, smiling, MARTIN begins to revolve. Lights out.)

(Lights up. An oppressive green. MARTIN, in his normal clothes, and MRS FARACLOUGH are sitting in the chairs. The stool is on one side of the stage. The record player is silent. The chairs are side by side. MARTIN and MRS FARACLOUGH both have huge wedding rings on.)

(Silence.)

MRS FARACLOUGH (looking at the stool): I wish they'd taken it away with them. It clutters the place up so.

MARTIN: They'll come back for it.

MRS FARACLOUGH: She's a rum woman. Every now and then she brings out a really nasty story. Spice, like cheese, she says.

MARTIN (whistles Bolero.)

MRS FARACLOUGH: She's repressed, of course.

MARTIN (whistles Bolero; stops): It takes genius.

(Whistles Bolero.)

MRS FARACLOUGH (annoyed): What takes genius?

MARTIN (whistles Bolero; stops): Breaking the shell.
(Whistles Bolero.)

MRS FARACLOUGH: I wish I'd known more about your
conversation before we'd got married. It was only the
monologues you had the gift for then, not the non-
sequiturs.

MARTIN (whistles Bolero.)

MRS FARACLOUGH (jumping up): Oh my God!

MARTIN (whistles Bolero.)

MRS FARACLOUGH: For God's sake Martin!

(MARTIN gets up whistling Bolero, and dances to it. He
stops whistling but continues dancing.)

MARTIN: People who break through their repressions are
geniuses.

(He whistles Bolero.)

MRS FARACLOUGH: Oh.

MARTIN (he stops whistling): That isn't a non-sequitur, I
don't think.

(He whistles Bolero.)

MRS FARACLOUGH: No.

(MARTIN stops dancing, stops whistling and looks at her.
He goes to the record player and puts on Bolero. They
dance first together, and then apart. They talk as they
dance.)

Anyway, she's a funny woman.

MARTIN (to the music): A funny woman.

(He repeats the phrase several times.)

MRS FARACLOUGH: Really smutty at times. Nothing
coarse about her.

MARTIN (again to the music): Not coarse at all, smutty
tales, smutty tales.

MRS FARACLOUGH: And she calls me smutty.

MARTIN (not in time to the music): The sociology of termin-
ology is fascinating.

MRS FARACLOUGH (going to turn off the record player):
Yet you've got to give it to her. She's a clean liver.

(The record is now off.)

MARTIN: She wanted to marry me. I found that pretty
disgusting.

(He goes to MRS FARACLOUGH. They kiss passionately.
They part.)

MRS FARACLOUGH: She'll be all right with Bowhorn.

MARTIN: You'd 've been all right with Bowhorn.
Financially.

MRS FARACLOUGH: Money isn't everything.

(They kiss again, passionately. They part.)

MARTIN: I don't seem to be able to get worked up.

MRS FARACLOUGH: No.

(They both sit down.)

MARTIN: Not even that. I wonder if Bowhorn gets worked
up.

MRS FARACLOUGH: Not much.

MARTIN: You're not really coarse, you know. Not what
I'd thought of as coarse.

MRS FARACLOUGH (flabbergasted): Are you talking to me?

MARTIN: You wash all over for one thing.

MRS FARACLOUGH: I should think so!

MARTIN: You're not as energetic as I'd imagined, either.

MRS FARACLOUGH (disbelieving): What?

MARTIN: I should have thought you'd have lingered on it
more, too.

MRS FARACLOUGH: It's not true!

MARTIN: And then, I don't know. You're smutty, too, in a
way. Nasty little stories, some of yours.

MRS FARACLOUGH: This is ridiculous!

MARTIN: It's disappointing.

MRS FARACLOUGH: Dis - Well, just you ask Brimley if
he's disappointed or not!

MARTIN: He's still asleep.

MRS FARACLOUGH: And why? And if that isn't evidence of coarseness, what is?

MARTIN: Oh, you're efficient all right. Coarse just isn't a word I associate with your thighs, though. And your bottom is too small.

MRS FARACLOUGH (gasps, speechless.)

(She leaps up, puts on Bolero very loud, seizes MARTIN and bears him behind the chairs. He smiles. Evidence of energetic activity.)

(MR BOWHORN runs on as if pursued. He goes as if to hide behind the chairs, sees what is happening, tries to move away, appears held, is dragged down. MARTIN gets up dressed only in his trousers, and shoes. He looks very cross. MISS PARTLIP runs on she sees MARTIN in undress and shrieking hides her eyes. He taps her on the shoulder and leads her behind the chair, pointing out what is happening there. She shrieks and begins hitting someone. MR BOWHORN gets up and runs out, dressed only in his trousers. MISS PARTLIP tries to follow him. She appears stuck. She is dragged down. She cries for help. MARTIN and MR BOWHORN watch, surprised. She disappears. MARTIN turns off the music. Silence.)

MARTIN: How many people were behind there?

MR BOWHORN: Dozens.

MARTIN: This is a fine moment if you like.

MR BOWHORN: A dreadful moment.

MARTIN: Are you married yet?

MR BOWHORN: We couldn't face it, dear boy.

MARTIN: You may have done the right thing. It's certainly not what I expected.

MR BOWHORN: Made a bloomer, have you?

MARTIN: I always used to say that if you went into things with your eyes open you had nothing to fear. However, who can be sure he has his eyes open?

MR BOWHORN: Me.

MARTIN: Oh?

MR BOWHORN: I've always been able to see things clearly.
That's been my outstanding characteristic.

MARTIN (annoyed): It's hard to believe your eyes work
better than mine.

MR BOWHORN: Yet you're married and I'm not.

MARTIN (annoyed and definite): You're not the prophetic
type.

MR BOWHORN: Oh, I don't know.

MARTIN (annoyed): You're not the prophetic type! I know
it.

MR BOWHORN: Now Martin, don't be obstinate.

MARTIN: If you'd been after Fanny Faraclough instead of
Miss Partlip you'd be married now! There!

MR BOWHORN: Fanny's not my kind of girl.

MARTIN: Oh?

MR BOWHORN: We couldn't share the finer things of life,
like crazy paving.

MARTIN: She'd love crazy paving. She's stupid enough for
anything.

MR BOWHORN: What?

MARTIN: Well, don't you think she's stupid?

MR BOWHORN: Well, now you mention it ...

MARTIN: No, before I mentioned it, did you think she was
stupid?

MR BOWHORN (after pause): Personally, I can think of no
greater work to the glory of man than a crazy paving
path threading across a well-trimmed lawn. A matter
of taste, I suppose.

MARTIN: Crap.

MR BOWHORN: Perhaps your eyes aren't as fully open as
you'd like to believe, Martin.

MARTIN: I couldn't bear them to be any further open than
they are. They reveal terrible things to me, like being
married to an unintelligent woman, who doesn't know the
difference between amusement and pleasure. (Angry):
I'm stuck with Fanny Faraclough by means of this great
ring, knotted on my finger, and I long for the mind of a

revolutionary to crash my way forward to the positive position!

MR BOWHORN: What position is that?

MARTIN: The state of grace, granted to few, when all the lines pass through you and you see the way. The mind is conscious, the body lithe, the emotions happily at work, and there's no weight that can't be moved, no organisation that isn't flexible, and in this position you go forward using your mind, your body, your emotions, deploying everything correctly, and each evening you feel blissfully tired. That's the positive position.

MR BOWHORN: That's right, Martin! Sometimes I wonder if I haven't quite misjudged you.

MARTIN: The mind of a revolutionary.

MR BOWHORN: A Karl Marx, a Robespierre, a Benjamin Franklin .....

(Pause. He looks down at his trousers.)

MARTIN (gloomy): You're probably right.

MR BOWHORN: So marriage after all doesn't suit you?

MARTIN: No.

(He turns to look at his chairs.)

I'd like to take my chairs away and go.

MR BOWHORN (turning to the chairs): I don't advise that just now.

MARTIN: No.

(Turning back): The trouble is, I can't converse with her.

MR BOWHORN (turning back): You may be able to in time.

MARTIN: And she's so .... far from what she thinks she is.

MR BOWHORN: How sad.

MARTIN: I'd like to sit down, but it seems permissive to do so.

MR BOWHORN: One is either permissive or one condemns. If one isn't one, one is the other. To stand is to be indecisive.

(He sits down.)

MARTIN: No!

(MR BOWHORN leaps up.)

MR BOWHORN: What?

MARTIN: I - I find it very disturbing to see you doing that with heaven knows what going on behind you.

(MR BOWHORN sits again.)

MR BOWHORN: Come, Martin, your attitude is hardly realistic.

(MARTIN stands confused.)

MR BOWHORN: What happened to that fancy dress?

MARTIN: You didn't imagine I could get married in it, did you?

MR BOWHORN: No.

(Pause.)

MARTIN: I wish someone would appear so we knew where we were.

MR BOWHORN: They will. In the meantime, enjoy the peace.

(Pause.)

(Some one starts whistling Pop Goes The Weasel. It is BRIMLEY, who, still whistling, slowly emerges from behind the chairs.)

(He comes forward and smiles at MARTIN and MR BOWHORN.)

MARTIN: You! I might've guessed.

MR BOWHORN: I thought you were asleep, Brimley.

BRIMLEY: I'm awake now.

MARTIN: Eavesdropping.

BRIMLEY: Oh no.

(He is putting on L'Apres-Midi d'un Faune.)

MR BOWHORN: Brimley's an enterprising fellow.

BRIMLEY: A one, as Mrs Faraclough so warmly puts it.

(Music plays. Pause.)

MARTIN: Well, I don't trust him.

BRIMLEY (listening to the music): Sh.

MARTIN: I don't.

BRIMLEY: Just listen to the music, then, and wait.

(Pause. MISS PARTLIP rises from the chairs.)

MISS PARTLIP: Is no-one going to do anything?

MR BOWHORN: Just let things take their course, Miss Partlip.

MISS PARTLIP: Martin?

MARTIN: I don't trust him, that's all.

MISS PARTLIP (near tears): I need action, Martin.

MARTIN: Miss Partlip, let me urge you, whatever you do, to test the intellect of your partner before you embark on anything so rash as marriage.

BRIMLEY: Made a bloomer, have you, Martin?

MR BOWHORN: Yes, he's made a bloomer.

MISS PARTLIP: Martin?

MARTIN: Miss Partlip, keep away.

MRS FARACLOUGH (behind the chairs): Elizabeth, leave off.

MARTIN (to MRS FARACLOUGH): Come out!

MRS FARACLOUGH: No!

MISS PARTLIP: Am I to be left alone?

MARTIN: Yes!

MR BOWHORN: My dear Miss Partlip, we've been through this already and we decided there wasn't any opportunity for ...

MISS PARTLIP: I'm soiled!

MARTIN: What do you mean?

MR BOWHORN: Don't ask.

BRIMLEY: The word is entirely relative. So, Martin's made a bloomer. Well, well, well. Have you made a bloomer, Fanny?

MRS FARACLOUGH (behind the chair): No.

BRIMLEY: If you'd made a bloomer, we'd be free to start all over again.

(Awkward pause. BRIMLEY stops the record. The lights begin to turn wishy-washy pale.)

MRS FARACLOUGH (getting up): Martin is mine. We'll work on it.

MARTIN: Never! I don't intend to compromise myself with you. I'm getting a divorce.

MRS FARACLOUGH: You can't! I'm good at marriage!

MARTIN: You've been with him!

(He points at BRIMLEY.)

BRIMLEY: Quickly, quickly, quickly. We're going to have a country dance, and everyone is going to like it.

(He puts it on.)

MARTIN: She has, Brimley.

BRIMLEY: Dance, Martin.

MISS PARTLIP: Dear Martin.

MARTIN: She's been with him, I know it.

MISS PARTLIP: Put your funny clothes on.

MARTIN: No. She's been with him.

MRS FARACLOUGH: Join the dance, Martin.

MARTIN: No!

MRS FARACLOUGH: And keep your bloody mouth shut.

MARTIN: But...

BRIMLEY: Nothing, Martin. Quickly, quickly, quickly.

MR BOWHORN: Come on Martin. Don't be so extraordinary.

(All dance an English country dance, such as Tam Pate. Suddenly MARTIN breaks away and gets on a chair.)

MARTIN: I'm going to get a divorce! I'm going to get a divorce!

(He keeps on until he leaves the stage.)

MRS FARACLOUGH (pulling at him): You're doing no such thing.

MISS PARTLIP (climbing the other chair): Now, Martin, you mustn't be upset.

MRS FARACLOUGH (pushing her off): Get off, you big fat virgin!

MISS PARTLIP (off the chair, perforce): Oh you nasty woman.

MRS FARACLOUGH: Don't you try to get your hands on Martin, because he's mine and he's enjoying it, and no-one's going to say he isn't.

(MARTIN has got off the chair still shouting and disappears, pushing the chair off as well.)

You bring that bloody chair back, you silly little runt.

(She goes off. BOWHORN and BRIMLEY have been dancing on sedately. Now BRIMLEY draws MISS PARTLIP into the dance to replace him. He picks up MARTIN's clothes and hurls them into the wings. He then follows the other two off, wheeling the second chair. MISS PARTLIP dances on very worried; MR BOWHORN in a reverie. Noises off of chairs being destroyed.)

MRS FARACLOUGH (off): Brimley stop it!

(Then, delighted by something): Ooooh!
(Then she giggles.)

(Bits of MARTIN's costume are thrown in tatters on to the stage.)

(The gramophone runs down. Silence. Then MARTIN's trousers are flung on to the stage. MISS PARTLIP is amazed. Silence.)

MISS PARTLIP: He was such a polite person. He reminded me of the pier keeper at Folkestone when I was little. "Come along, little lady", he used to say. "If I hide my eyes, perhaps I won't see you creep through, and perhaps I won't charge the little lady for a ticket." It was very important, even then, that a man should call me little. There was something like that about Martin.

BRIMLEY (off): Mr Bowen!

MR BOWHORN: What? Oh. That's me. Yes?

BRIMLEY: We're coming, Mr Bowen.

(Enter BRIMLEY pushing MRS FARACLOUGH on a sofa - a very modern one. MRS FARACLOUGH is happy and giggling.)

BRIMLEY: There. I couldn't just leave us all with nothing to sit on.

MISS PARTLIP (near tears): Where's the boy?

BRIMLEY: Boy? What boy?

MISS PARTLIP: I won't ask again. Just tell me where he is.

BRIMLEY: I don't know who you're talking about.

MR BOWHORN: Bourne, actually, is the intimate family pronunciation.

BRIMLEY: Bourne. Thank you so much.

MISS PARTLIP: I see.

BRIMLEY: We'd like to invite you to our wedding, wouldn't we Fanny.

MRS FARACLOUGH (laughs): One long round of marriage, eh Miss Partlip?

(MISS PARTLIP is near to tears.)

BRIMLEY: And you? What about you?

(Silence.)

We'll wait for you.

(BRIMLEY and MRS FARACLOUGH embrace on the sofa.)

MISS PARTLIP (near tears): It's no use being nostalgic, I suppose.

MR BOWHORN: Not a bit.

MISS PARTLIP (near tears): We've got to face the facts.

MR BOWHORN: Yes.

MISS PARTLIP (crying): Then we'd better settle to it, Edward. It will be a double marriage, neat as anything.

MR BOWHORN: You mean us? Oh, I don't think I could quite agree ...

BRIMLEY: I'm sure you could, Mr Bourne.

MR BOWHORN: You think ...

BRIMLEY: I'm sure.

MR BOWHORN: Then ... Elizabeth, the trusted friend of whom....

MISS PARTLIP (crying): Yes, Edward. I'll have you.

BRIMLEY: How nice. Now we can all live happily ever after.

(BRIMLEY and MRS FARACLOUGH embrace very fully.
MR BOWHORN holds MISS PARTLIP's hand. She cries.)

MR BOWHORN: There, there, there, there, there, there, there.

CURTAIN

John Mortimer	LUNCH HOUR and Other Plays
	TWO STARS FOR COMFORT
	THE JUDGE
Joe Orton	LOOT
Harold Pinter	THE BIRTHDAY PARTY
	THE ROOM AND THE DUMB WAITER
	THE CARETAKER
	A SLIGHT ACHE and Other Plays
	THE COLLECTION AND THE LOVER
	THE HOMECOMING
	TEA PARTY and Other Plays
Jean-Paul Sartre	CRIME PASSIONNEL
Theatre Workshop and Charles Chilton	OH WHAT A LOVELY WAR

Methuen's Theatre Classics

Euripides an English version by Neil Curry	THE TROJAN WOMEN
Adapted by Gordon Honeycombe from five cycles of Mystery Plays	THE REDEMPTION
Goethe adapted by John Arden	IRONHAND
Ibsen translated by Michael Meyer	BRAND
	THE WILD DUCK
	HEDDA GABLER
	THE MASTER BUILDER
Strindberg translated by Michael Meyer	MISS JULIE
Wilde	LADY WINDERMERE'S FAN
	THE IMPORTANCE OF BEING EARNEST

Other Plays from Methuen

Jean Anouilh   COLLECTED PLAYS VOLUME I
(The Ermine, Thieves' Carnival,
Restless Heart, Traveller without
Luggage, Dinner with the Family)
COLLECTED PLAYS VOLUME II
(Time Remembered, Point of Departure,
Antigone, Romeo and Jeanette, Medea)

Bertolt Brecht   PLAYS VOLUME I
(The Caucasian Chalk Circle, The
Threepenny Opera, The Trial of
Lucullus, The Life of Galileo)
PLAYS VOLUME II
(Mother Courage, St Joan of the
Stockyards, The Good Person of
Szechwan)

Max Frisch   THREE PLAYS
(The Fire Raisers, Count Oederland,
Andorra)

Jean Giraudoux   PLAYS VOLUME I
(Tiger at the Gates, Duel of Angels,
Judith)
PLAYS VOLUME II
(Amphitryon, Intermezzo, Ondine)

John Millington Synge   PLAYS AND POEMS